Your Amazing Itty Bitty Financial Wisdom Book

15 Steps to Build, Preserve, & Protect Your Wealth

Besides your health, your finances are the backbone of your life. Everyone needs to be prepared for what life might bring: your children's education, retirement, illness, disability, and even death.

Having insurance policies can help keep you and your family safe. Life insurance is a tool that can be used during life as well as at the end of life. You can draw upon it as you need.

Everyone is unique and has different needs. In this Itty Bitty™ book, Bronwyn L. Martin, using available products and portfolios, gives you the financial wisdom to make wise choices for your family's future.

In this book you will learn:

- Investment strategies
- How to prepare for retirement
- How to take care of taxes
- And so much more.

Be financially empowered as life throws you curve balls and pick up a copy of this must-read Itty Bitty™ book today.

Your Amazing Itty Bitty™ Financial Wisdom Book

15 Steps to Build, Preserve, and Protect Your Wealth

Bronwyn L. Martin,
PhD, MBA, ChFC®,
CLU®, AEP®

Published by Itty Bitty™ Publishing
A subsidiary of S & P Productions, Inc.

Printed in the United States of America

Itty Bitty Publishing
311 Main Street, Suite D
El Segundo, CA 90245
(310) 640-8885

ISBN: 978-1-7329566-5-0

This information is for educational purposes only
and is not intended as a substitute for any legal,
financial, or tax advice. Seek the advice of an
attorney, a CPA, or a fee-only financial advisor if
such service is needed.

Dedication

This book is dedicated to those who want to be more financially successful, who may be embarrassed to ask, but still seek out advice. I hope these tidbits of information will help you reach out to a professional to help you with your specific situations and your specific goals.

Stop by our Itty Bitty™ website to find
interesting blog entries regarding wealth

www.IttyBittyPublishing.com

Or contact Dr. Bronwyn L. Martin at:

610.453.7215

Table of Contents

Introduction

There is a broad range of topics here because I've found over the years that they are important topics to the clients I have worked with and helped. They range in age from 19 to 96, but are mostly between—30-85 years of age. These seem to be the years when people start to make a decent income, look to buy their first home, start a family, consider starting their own business, and retire early. Or later. Those enjoying retirement may need to recreate their paycheck to pass on their hard-earned money and assets to beneficiaries and charities. And everyone needs to be prepared for the things we hate to think about: disability and death.

I believe in every product mentioned here. As I say to my clients, I wouldn't have you invested in anything I wouldn't recommend to my mother. But the product and portfolio have to make sense for *your* situation. So, make sure you work with a professional who is objective and listens to you and what *you* want to achieve.

To your ongoing financial success—cheers!

Step 1
Why Do I Need Life Insurance if My Kids Have Graduated College?

Are you one of those people who thinks life insurance is only to provide enough money to pay off the mortgage and your children's education should you die young? Do you know how much college will cost by the time your children are ready for it?

1. Life insurance is a tool that can be used during life as well as at the end of life.
2. Permanent life insurance has a hidden treasure called cash value. This is a "forced" savings feature inside the premium.
3. If you pay the guideline premium instead of the minimum premium, the cash value accumulates and grows. Universal life and variable universal life insurance have this feature.
4. You can use the cash value to pay for things during your life: college, purchase of a home, retirement, anything!
5. The bigger the death benefit the bigger the cash value. Not only are you leaving money at your death, but you have also created a savings pool to use during life.

More About Why You Need Life Insurance

Yes, there is a hidden value to your life insurance. However, be aware of the risks if you use this as a source of cash flow.

- Don't take out all the cash value because you risk creating a taxable event.
- Don't use the cash value like your checking account.

If you currently have term insurance, talk with your insurance agent or financial advisor about converting some or all your term insurance to permanent insurance or adding permanent insurance to your financial plan.

- Review how the policy works
- Make sure the premium fits your budget

Step 2
Why Disability Insurance Coverage
Through Your Employer
May Not Be Enough

Your ability to earn an income is one of the most valuable assets you have.

1. Based on your current income and working until age 65, it's likely you will have earned over a million dollars.
2. Almost 90% of accidents and illnesses are not work-related.
3. If you become disabled, would you have enough income to meet your financial obligations? Would you need to make lifestyle changes for yourself or your family? Would you be able to pay uncovered medical costs?
4. When you investigate the details of most employer-sponsored group benefits, you will find they typically don't include bonuses or incentive compensation income.
5. To supplement employer coverage, consider an individual disability income insurance policy which likely won't cost more than 2% of your total insurable income.

More About Disability Insurance Coverage

Your employer coverage is not enough to cover your base salary because these policies are typically capped at 60% of your gross income and doesn't cover bonus income or incentive compensation.

- Talk to your financial planner about getting additional coverage.
- Consider whether current assets will cover the cost of an extended illness or sickness. (Six years is the average claim length[1]).
- Review the features of the policy for the following features:
    - Partial disability coverage: what is covered and what isn't.
    - Own occupation definition: your *specific* occupation; not *any* occupation as defined by the Social Security Act[2].
    - Waiver of premium: how it protects your policy.
    - Noncancelable and guaranteed renewable policies cannot be canceled for any reason.
- Men have a 43% chance of becoming seriously disabled during their working years; women have a 54% chance[3].

Step 3
Should I Invest in a 529 Plan for My Children's Education?

529 plans are tax-advantaged education savings plans that cover more than you think they do.

1. A 529 plan is a great idea if used to pay for tuition and college fees at any accredited school or graduate school.
2. A 529 plan can be used for student loan repayment.
3. It can also be used for K-12 expenses up to $10,000/year.

Grandparents can be involved as well. What a great gift from them for your child's future!

1. A 529 plan is a great way to contribute to a grandchild; their 529 account doesn't impact the estimated family contribution (EFC) if your child needs financial aid.
2. Earnings from 529 plans accrue tax deferred and are tax free if used per step one above.
3. Know the differences* between 529 savings plans and 529 prepaid tuition plans.

More About Investing in a 529 Plan

It's important to know there are rules to follow when using a 529 plan. The good news is they're easier than you think.

- You can always pay for college costs with other types of accounts, or just cash flow.
- Be sure you're not depleting your retirement savings to fund an education.
- Consult with your financial advisor for additional help on funding college costs.
- Consult your tax advisor for help on 529 contributions, distributions, and gifting exclusions.

*529 Savings plans are designed to help families set aside funds for future education expenses.
529 Prepaid plans are more restrictive than 529 savings plans but prepay your child's future college tuition.

Step 4
What Is Umbrella Insurance, and Do I Need It?

Umbrella Insurance (UI) is excess coverage to help cover liability expenses.

UI:

1. It provides liability protection above and beyond your basic homeowner/renter and auto insurance policies.
2. If you're sued, a large judgment could wipe you out financially.

How does umbrella coverage work? Let's say you have $300,000 in auto coverage and you're facing an $800,000 auto lawsuit. You could owe $500,000 out of pocket, but with $1M umbrella coverage, you'd owe nothing ($0).

Reasons to Buy Umbrella Insurance

Surprisingly, your property and casualty insurance agent may never have mentioned umbrella insurance.

Following are some reasons you might want to consider having this type of coverage.

- A guest is injured at a party in your house or pool.
- A car accident leads to multiple injuries.
- Someone accuses you of libel, slander, or defamation of character.
- A personal lawsuit is brought against you.

Your property and casualty insurance provider can explain how umbrella insurance protects you, and under what circumstances.

Step 5
What If I Lose My Job?

Losing your job, especially unexpectedly, can be crushing emotionally and financially.

1. Always be prepared for such a situation by having cash reserves for core expenses equivalent to three to six months' income.
2. Look for a new job at the same or higher level of pay.
3. Be sure to look closely at the benefits of the prospective new company.
4. Roll your 401k over into an IRA.
5. Be aware that you no longer have either employer-provided life insurance or disability insurance coverage.

How to Be Better Prepared if You Lose Your Job

Here are a few ideas to help soften the blow should the unexpected happen.

- Have life and disability insurance policies not connected to your workplace. Your financial advisor can help you see the gap between employer-provided coverages and what amount you need in supplemental insurance should you lose your job. In the event that this does happen, you still have this private insurance.
- Have a home equity line of credit (HELOC) in place. You need this LOC in place *before* you become unemployed.
    - A HELOC is like having a credit card: you pay the expenses once you use the account. Not to be confused with a home loan where re-payment is due immediately whether you have used the money or not.

Step 6
To Trust or Not to Trust

A trust is a legal entity that holds assets for the benefit of another and can also hold various types of assets. There are many types of trusts, each designed for a specific purpose.

1. Trusts are often used to minimize estate taxes.
2. Trusts help you avoid both the expense and delay of probating a will and settling your estate.
3. Probate* delays the transfer of your assets and incurs possible attorney and executor fees to be paid out of your estate, not to mention the time the executor of your estate must deal with the delays, court appearances, meetings with attorneys and other advisors.
4. Trusts can provide assets for your children until they are grown or mature.
5. A trust can support you in the event of incapacity.

*Probate is a court-supervised process that winds up your financial affairs after your death, taking place in the state where you were at the time of your death, and can take years.

Three Common Types of Trusts

As previously mentioned, there are many kinds of trusts. Those most commonly used may include one or all of the following:

- Revocable or living trust: avoids probate, maintains control, and protects against incapacity.
- Irrevocable trust cannot be easily changed (i.e., beneficiaries or terms) and is frequently used to help reduce potential estate taxes.
- Testamentary trust arises upon the death of the testator, and which is specified in his or her will. A will may contain more than one testamentary trust and may address all or any portion of the estate.

Consult with your estate planning attorney.

Step 7
Why Should I Give to Charity?

Being generous is a humanitarian gesture that makes you feel good. You can give now, throughout your life, and at your death.

1. Gifts can be given outright, or you can use a trust for distributions during your lifetime.
2. You can name a charity as a beneficiary in your will or designate a charity as a beneficiary of your retirement plan or life insurance policy.

Besides feeling good about your generosity, there are other benefits listed below.

1. The designated charity benefits immediately and exclusively with outright gifts. You get both immediate income tax and gift tax deductions.
2. Gifts at your death provide both income and estate tax deductions for your estate.
3. Giving away your retirement plan eliminates you and your heirs from paying taxes on distributions.

Pointers on Giving

You can imagine that giving away a large amount of money could be a red flag to the IRS. So, take note of the following tax-related pointers.

- To get a tax deduction, make sure the charity is qualified according to the IRS.
- Get written receipts for cash donations or donated property.
- Life insurance is a great way to give away a lot of money to charity at a much lower cost to you.

Charitable trusts are most commonly used in the form of charitable lead trusts (CLT) and charitable remainder trusts (CRT).

A CLT pays income to your chosen charity for a certain period of years after your death. Once that period is up, the trust principal passes to your family members or other heirs.

A CRT pays income to your family members or other heirs for a certain period of years after your death or for the lifetime of one or more beneficiaries. Then the principal goes to your favorite charity.

For both types of trusts, the dollar amount given to charity (the income or the remainder) is what produces the estate tax charitable deduction for you.

Step 8
Who Cares If I Don't Name Beneficiaries on My Retirement Accounts?

Your beneficiaries will care! Many people think that all assets automatically go to a surviving spouse, and then surviving children at your death. That is not necessarily the case.

1. Name the person or persons you want to receive your death benefits from your life insurance and annuity policies; both your group policy and individually owned policies.
2. Name the person or persons you want to receive your retirement assets and your IRA(s).
3. Be aware that your written will does not override the beneficiaries listed on these types of accounts.

A familiar but unfortunate scenario is that an ex-spouse is listed as the primary beneficiary on a retirement account or life insurance policy and the new spouse gets no assets at the death of the account owner.

A Few Reasons to Check on Your Beneficiaries

Check your designated beneficiaries every few years and when a change happens in your life, i.e., marriage, divorce, a new child.

- Your primary beneficiary may have died, or you no longer want them named as a beneficiary.
- Your secondary beneficiaries could automatically become your primary ones. Take immediate action if that is not what you want.

If you don't name a beneficiary, the account ends up in your probate estate, thus delaying the transfer of the assets and incurring possible attorney and executor fees. If you name your estate as your beneficiary, the court will decide who your beneficiary is, which can be a tax nightmare for that person.

- Name beneficiaries: people or charities
- Review beneficiaries regularly

Step 9
What if I Get an Inheritance?

You will naturally mourn the loss of a close relative, but at the same time, you may feel guilty about your excitement at getting an inheritance. Take time to figure out what you want to do with your windfall.

These following guidelines will help you establish a baseline of financial well-being:

1. Keep aside (in cash) any inheritance taxes you may have to pay. Check with your estate executor.
2. Make sure your cash reserve is at least a three-month supply of your fixed (not discretionary) expenses.
3. Pay off as much consumer debt as possible: credit card debt, school loans, auto loans, etc.

What Do I Do if There's Inheritance Money Left Over?

The deceased may have wanted to help you get through grad school, take the vacation of your dreams, buy a house, or help fund your retirement.

People leave money at their death to help provide for loved ones and to thank specific people. Individuals don't leave you money because they have to—it's strictly discretionary.

A few cautions about your newly acquired windfall:

- Don't lend away your new money; it's unlikely you will get it back.
- This is the time to start wise financial planning.

Step 10
What if I'm Forced to Retire?

You may know people who have been forced out of their jobs because of downsizing or the need to take care of an aging parent or grandparent. So, if you're confronted with this "opportunity," what will you do?

1. Assess all your available assets.
2. Determine whether you still need to work.
3. Position your investments appropriately.

Carefully determine whether you really have enough money on hand to meet your income needs, not just for the immediate future, but throughout your retirement.

1. If you can retire, you may need to reduce your investment risk profile.
2. Money needed for income in the next one to three years should be held in relatively safe investments such as cash or short-term bonds.

Don't Forget About Medical Insurance From an Employer

The transition to retirement is one of the most important financial periods of your life.

Check into your health care options.

- If you are 65 or older, you have the option to enroll in Medicare. If not, you'll need to consider other options.
- See if your employer extends health care coverage for a period of time (called COBRA, short for Consolidated Omnibus Budget Reconciliation Act), or if you have the option to pay to maintain current coverage.
- If you are married, you may possibly be added to your spouse's coverage plan.
- If those choices aren't available, you can explore an individual healthcare policy, utilizing the Affordable Care Act Marketplace.

Step 11
Does Medicare Pay for Long-Term Care Costs?

Unfortunately, many people assume that Medicare will cover any LTC (long-term care) they might need. It is a mistaken belief that nursing home or at-home care will be taken care of.

1. Medicare covers the cost of medical care.
2. To be eligible for *Medicaid* to pay for long-term care costs, your income (SSI, pension, etc.) and assets must be within federal poverty guidelines: The income cap is about $2,500/month with assets not to exceed $2,000-$4,000.

Paying for long-term care costs:

1. You can use investments, assets, and income to cover these costs.
2. You can use the cash value of permanent life insurance (see Chapter 1), life insurance with a long-term care rider, or a hybrid annuity. A rider provides a benefit, like long-term care coverage.
3. You can use a reverse mortgage.

More About Paying for Long-term Care Costs

Additional ways to cover in-home care costs and nursing home costs:

- You can use a viatical* or lifetime settlement of existing life insurance.
- You can also use long-term care insurance.

You might need help to figure out long-term costs, especially the further away you estimate you are from incurring them.

- Talk with your financial advisor about planning for long-term care costs based on your age and your assets.
- Talk with your tax advisor about long-term care premium deductibility, taxation of benefits, and taxation of a lifetime settlement.

*Viatical is an arrangement whereby a person with a terminal illness sells their life insurance policy to a 3rd party for less than its mature value, in order to benefit from the proceeds while alive to pay for care, i.e., your $500,000 death benefit life policy is sold for $220,000, giving you immediate cash while alive.

Step 12
Aren't Annuities for Old People?

Because this chapter is devoted to annuities, you can safely guess that the answer is no, they're not just for old people. Annuities can be a great tool in your asset lineup. So, what are they and how do they work?

1. Money in annuities grows tax deferred. Taxes are deferred until you withdraw the money.
2. Annuities can have a guaranteed death benefit; your beneficiaries are guaranteed to receive at least what you invested.
3. Annuities can be used to create a guaranteed income for life.
4. Annuity payouts can continue to your spouse.

Numbers two through four above are reasons to envision an annuity inside an IRA even though you don't get a double tax-deferral benefit from utilizing both an annuity and an IRA.

More About Annuities

Unlike income limits placed on vehicles like IRAs or annual limits on contributions to 401k plans, neither limit applies to annuities. However, there are some reasons to make sure an annuity is the right fit at the time of purchase.

- You could be assessed a penalty if you withdraw more than 10% of your principal before the contract term is over.
- Growth is taxed at ordinary income rates, not long-term capital gain rates.

Like so many financial planning tools, there are many kinds of annuities with many kinds of riders (additional benefits at an extra cost). What is best for you depends on your situation and your goals. Annuities may or may not be suitable for you at this time.

Step 13
Taxes, Taxes, Taxes!

I've never met anyone who happily writes a check to the US Treasury. We pay taxes as US citizens, but we're always looking for legitimate ways to pay less. Here are some ideas:

1. Contribute to your retirement plan and max out your contribution.
2. Make contributions to a Roth IRA.
3. Contribute to an annuity or permanent life insurance.
4. Give money to a 501(c)3 charitable organization or a donor-advised fund.

If you qualify, consider the suggestions below.

1. Set up a schedule to exercise stock options and restricted stock units (RSUs) so you're not hit with a big tax bill next year. And make sure you exercise the RSU stock options before exiting the company! You forfeit them if laid off or you retire.
2. Invest in non-publicly traded real estate investment trusts (REITs), which aren't doubly taxed like corporate stock; they are pass-through entities. Always be sure you understand investment risks.

Taxes on Inherited Money

Your beneficiaries will have to pay "death taxes" on what you leave to them.

- Check with your state treasury for the tax amount that will be charged to your heirs.
- Typically, the value of the inheritance is the value of the investment at the date of death. This might be the time to sell and pay less in taxes on the inheritance.

Make sure your tax advisor, estate planner, and financial planner work together to help you with minimizing and delaying taxes.

Step 14
What Financial Planning Tools Should I Consider if I'm Self-Employed?

The tools you put in place will, of course, be based on where you are in your business setup: number of and type of employees (full-time, part-time), international, or domestic-based, etc.

Consider these points to include in your business planning as you start your business and it matures:

1. Keep your business and personal expenses and monies separate.
2. Be sure to maintain complete business records going back a minimum of three years in case of an IRS audit.
3. Set up your business as an LLC, S-corporation, or other type as recommended by your advisor.
4. Set up a retirement plan for yourself and your employees.
5. Consider buying business overhead insurance.
6. Create a tax strategy—you will need to pay estimated taxes and self-employment taxes on a quarterly basis.

The "Don'ts" of Having Your Own Business

- Don't forget to build your liquid savings since your income could change based on seasonality, the economy, and your need to grow—including additional staff and equipment.
- Don't use your retirement savings to start or fund your own business.
- Don't forget to enroll in a good health insurance plan if you're single or responsible for your spouse or children. Or see if you're eligible to be covered under your spouse's insurance.

Your tax and financial advisors can help you determine the type of business structure to implement.

Step 15
Real Estate as an Asset

Real estate is a hedge against inflation because it tends to keep pace with, or exceed, inflation in terms of appreciation. But some people can't stomach being a landlord. Here are some pointers about including real estate in your portfolio.

1. Your first investment property could be your business location for immediate equity in your business, as my dad told me.
2. Investment real estate has a shorter loan period and higher down payment when borrowing from a bank.
3. Make sure your rental income covers at least principal and interest (P&I), insurance, taxes, and repairs.
4. Anticipate a two-to-four-week vacancy after each tenant to clean and make repairs using the security deposit.
5. You can leverage the equity in your property once it has equity in it to buy the next property.
6. You can own real estate without being a landlord by buying into real estate investment trusts (REITs). Refer back to Step 13.

You Need a Team Behind the Scenes

Like most things, you need a team of people to count on.

- Find a realtor who understands you're buying an investment property and what your goal is, whether it's your first or tenth real estate purchase.
- Make sure you have a plumber, electrician, HVAC specialist, general contractor, and roofer you can count on. When there's a problem, you'll need reliable, trustworthy contractors to do the job right and at reasonable rates.

Consider getting a real estate license, even if only to be a referral agent where you negotiate a referral fee with the primary realtor.

Being a landlord can be a huge step. Talk it over with your significant other, parents, or friends who have already done this.

It's exciting and you might find you like it!

End Note References

[1] From a 2020 RiverSource Claims Report.
[2] https://www.ssa.gov/disabilityfacts/facts.html
[3] "Why Disability" booklet, published by National Underwrite

You've finished. Before you go...

Post/Share that you finished this book.

Please star rate this book.

Reviews are solid gold to writers. Please take a few minutes to give us some itty bitty feedback.

ABOUT THE AUTHOR

Bronwyn Martin earned two degrees at Boston University (BU) and spent time as a researcher at MIT. After earning her Ph.D. in biochemistry, at BU School of Medicine, the Australian native worked as a postdoctoral research fellow at both Harvard Medical School and the National Institutes of Health. While working as a medical writer, she enrolled in West Chester University's executive Master of Business Administration program and set up her financial planning practice in 2000, operating with offices in PA and MD.

Bronwyn has numerous publications in the science field and the financial planning industry. She has multiple designations in the financial planning arena that focus on specific topics. She has awards both for her excellence in the field as well as her contributions to the community.

If you enjoyed this Itty Bitty™ book you might also like…

- **Your Amazing Itty Bitty™ Financial Fitness Book** by Akemi Clauson

- **Your Amazing Itty Bitty™ "Before" Financial Checklist** by Marie Burns

- **Your Amazing Itty Bitty™ Blissful Real Estate Investing Book** by Moneeka Sawyer

Or any of the many Amazing Itty Bitty™ books available online at www.ittybittypublishing.com